Hope, Love & Science

By Becky Westhead

ISBN: 978-1-7646102-1-6

Written by Becky Westhead

Illustrations created by Becky Westhead

Hi! My name is Cooper.

I am so glad you're here.
I'm going to tell you
about how I came
into the big, bright world.

You see, my mum and dad
needed a little extra help
to make me.

Some very kind
and clever people
helped them
along the way.

Mum and dad wished for me for a very long time.
They hoped, waited, and dreamed,
but they realised they needed some extra help.
One day, they met with Dr Anju, who told them about
a special kind of help called IVF.

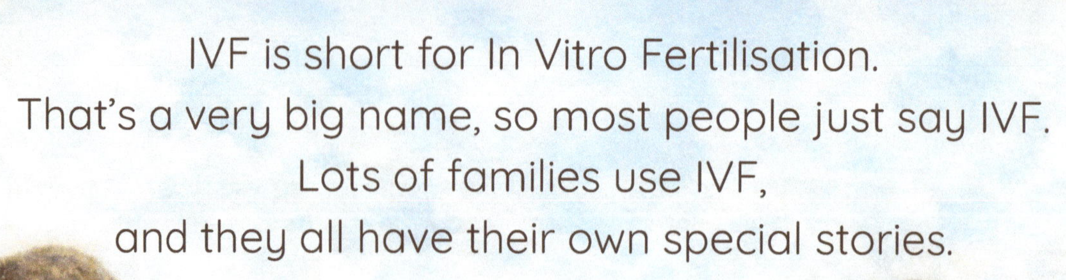

IVF is short for In Vitro Fertilisation.
That's a very big name, so most people just say IVF.
Lots of families use IVF,
and they all have their own special stories.

To get ready, mum and dad had
some important work to do.
Mum took special medicine and had tiny needles.
She didn't always feel brave —
so sometimes dad held her hand.

Little by little, mum found her courage.
One day she even did the needles all by herself. She was so excited to tell dad.
Dad was very proud of mum.
I was too — even though I was still so very tiny.

The medicine helped mum's eggs grow big and strong.

When the eggs were ready, Dr Anju gently collected them, with help from the caring nurses at the hospital.

Mum's special eggs were given to a scientist.
The scientist carefully brought mum's egg and dad's seed together in a laboratory.
That's where my story began.

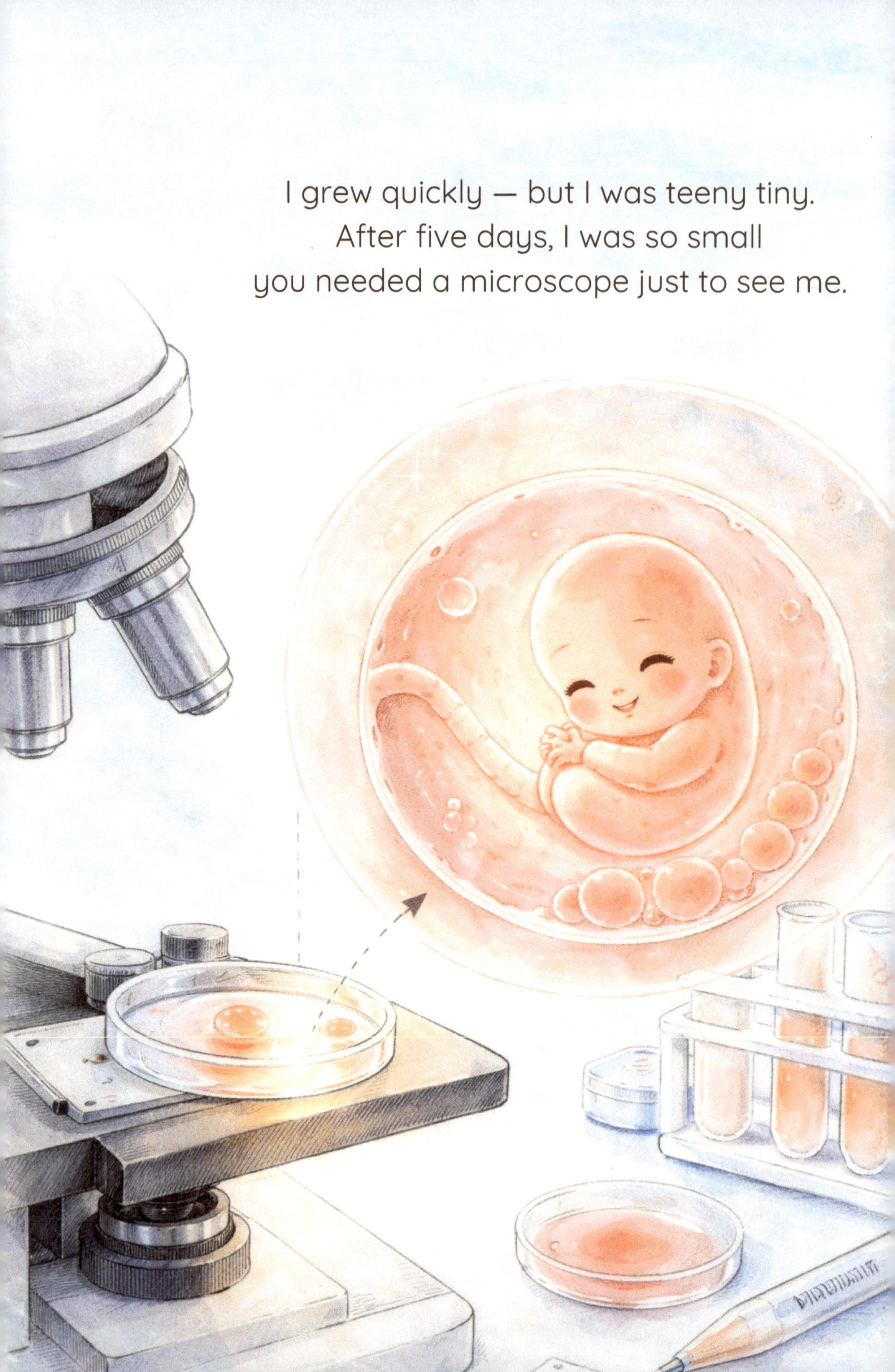

I grew quickly — but I was teeny tiny.
After five days, I was so small
you needed a microscope just to see me.

Then came a very important day.
The doctors and nurses carefully placed me into mum's tummy.
They used a special screen called an ultrasound to help guide me to the perfect spot.

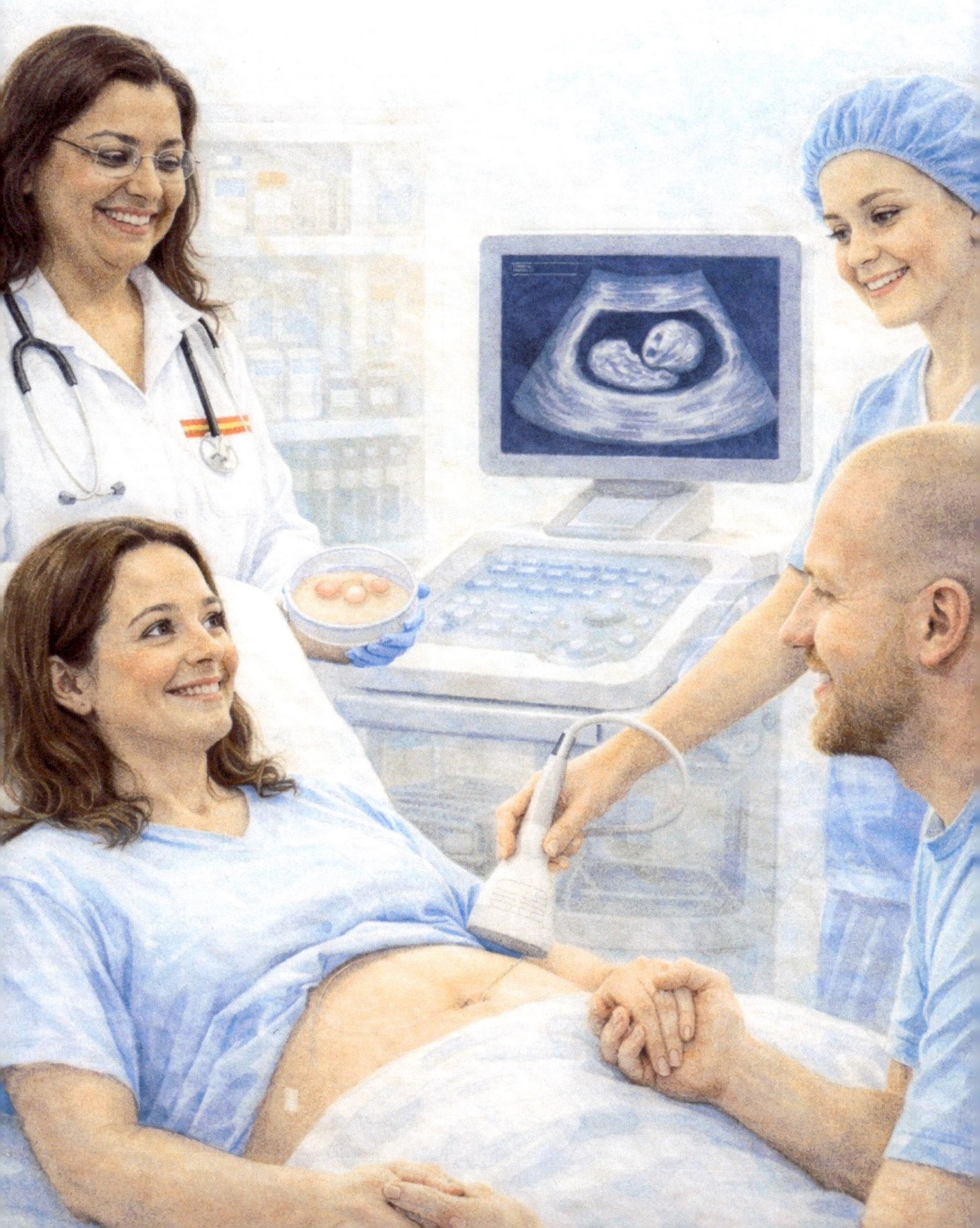

Afterwards, mum and dad went to get hot chips.
Mum said it was good luck.
I think she was right.

Two weeks later, mum had a special blood test.
She waited by the phone, feeling nervous.
Then the nurse called and said,
"Congratulations — you're having a baby."
Mum cried happy tears, and dad smiled the biggest smile.
And I stayed right there, safe and snug, growing every day.

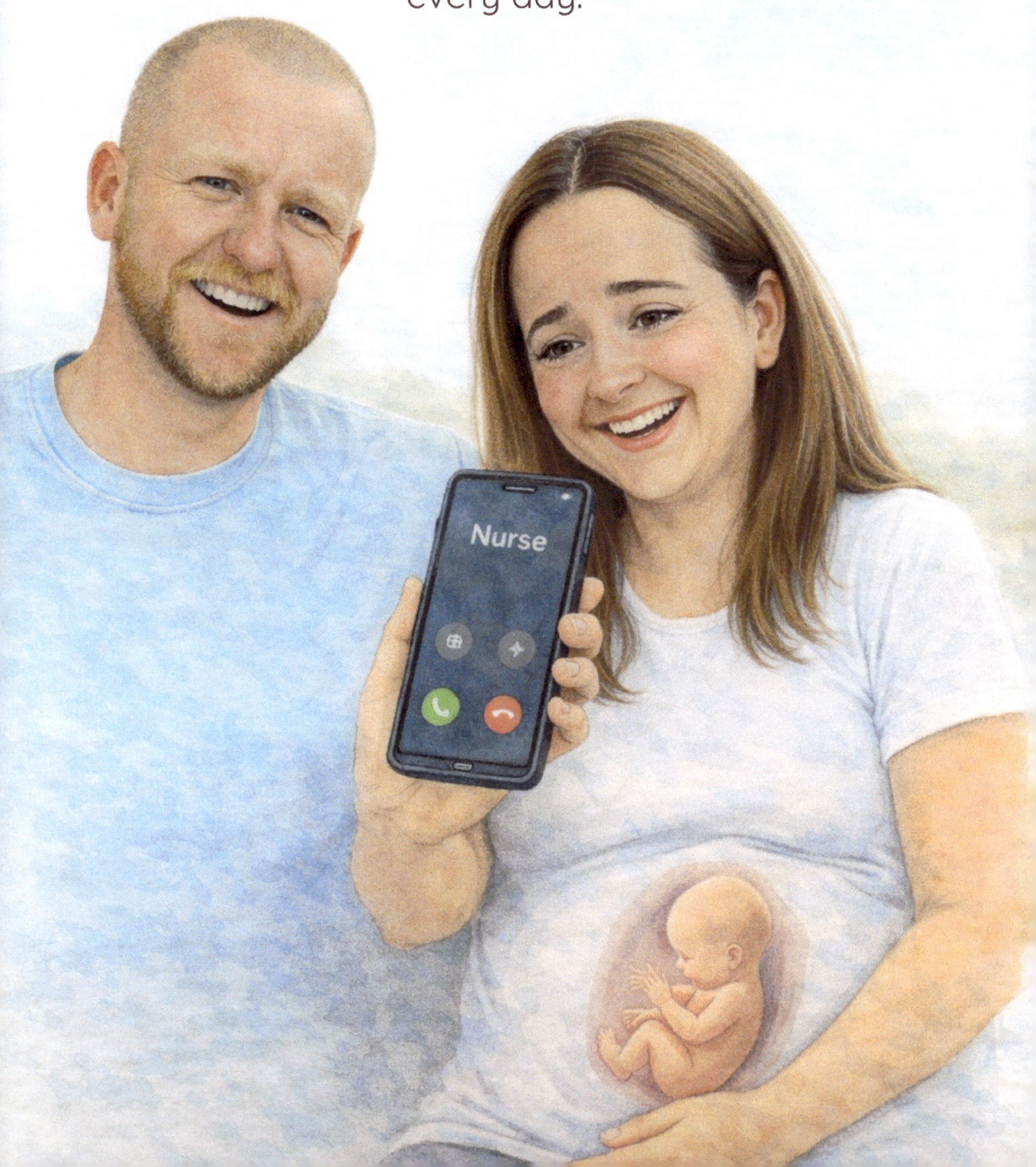

Mum and dad watched mum's tummy grow.
It started small... then grew bigger and bigger.
Sometimes I made mum feel sick,
but she didn't mind — she was happy I was growing.

One night on the couch, mum felt my tiny kicks.
She tried to get dad to feel them too –
but I was cheeky and stopped kicking right away.

Mum had to go get lot's of photo's of me.
These photo's were called ultrasounds.
They check to make sure I am growing.

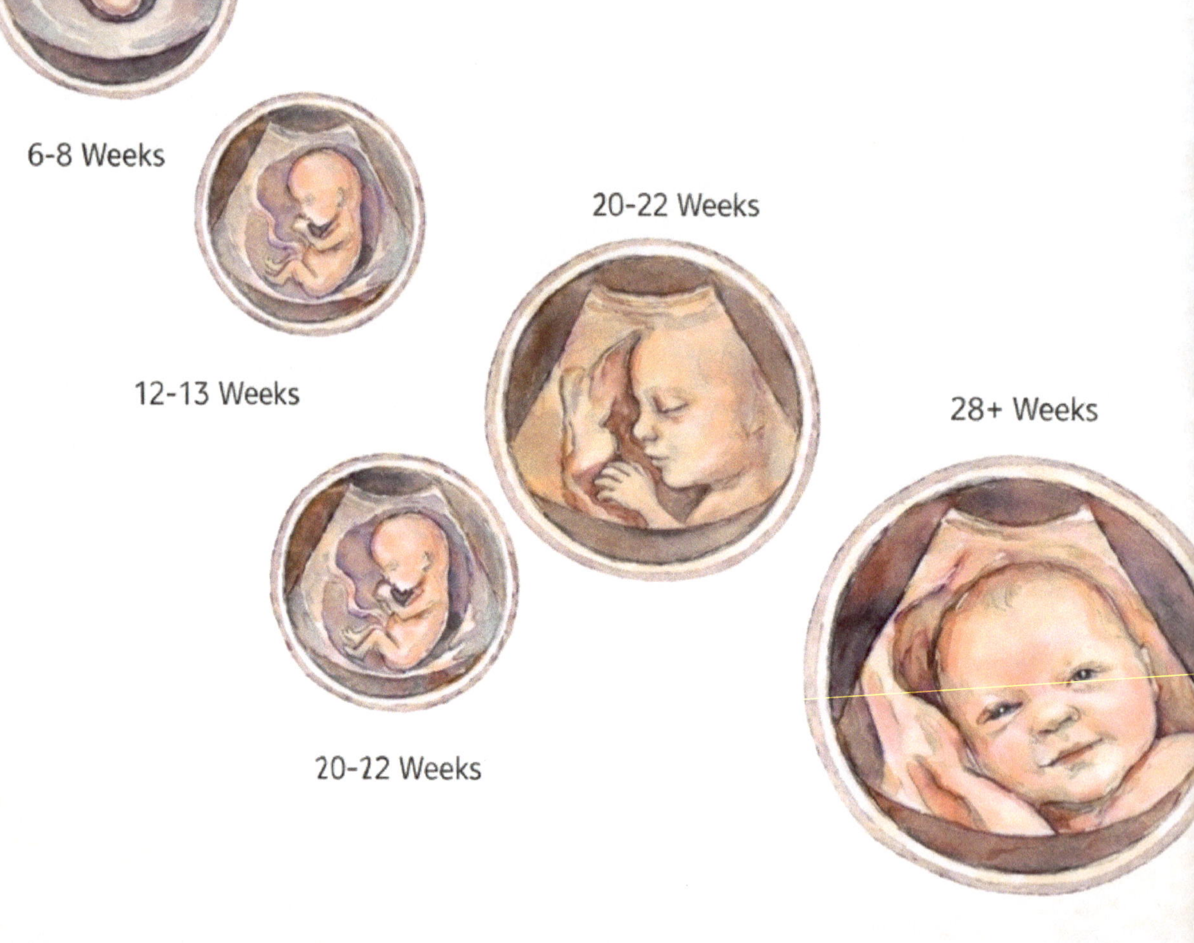

My aunties threw a special party for me
while I was still in mum's tummy.
My family and friends couldn't wait to meet me.

After many months, it was time for me to be born.
Lots of doctors and nurses helped me arrive safely.
After I was born, everyone checked to
make sure I was healthy.
Mum says I had big blue eyes, lots of hair,
and a little cry.

I think it's so cool that many people helped make me. Maybe you or someone you know is apart of our very cool IVF club too.

To our miracle baby Cooper.

I dedicate this book to you and all the happiness
you have brought us in what was such a challenging time.

I love you very much

Love Mum.

A special thanks to Dr Anju and The Monash Team
for supporting us on our IVF journey.

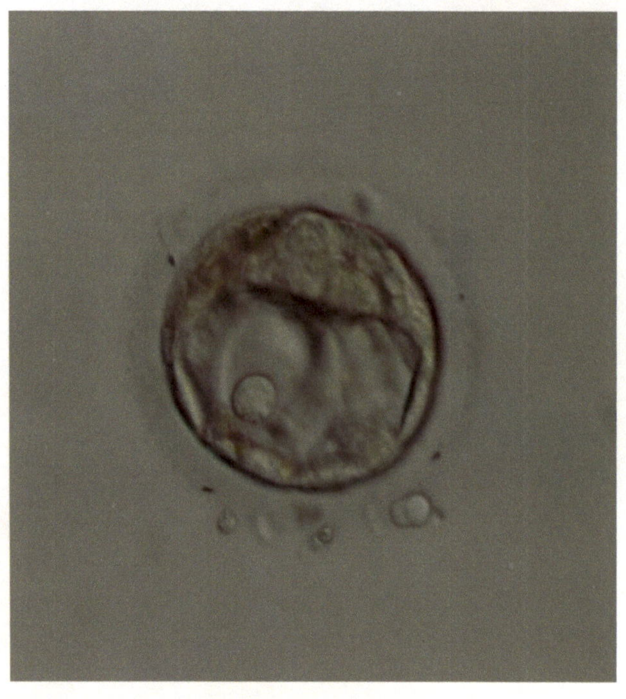

Cooper's first photo

www.ingramcontent.com/pod-product-compliance
Lightning Source LLC
LaVergne TN
LVHW070209110826
845147LV00002B/540

9781764610216